Peter Haswell

# Whales

*Illustrated by*
*Steve White*

**OXFORD**
UNIVERSITY PRESS

For Jack, Millie, Fabian, and Joshua–P.H.

# OXFORD
### UNIVERSITY PRESS

Great Clarendon Street, Oxford OX2 6DP

Oxford University Press is a department of the University of Oxford.
It furthers the University's objective of excellence in research, scholarship,
and education by publishing worldwide in

Oxford  New York

Athens  Auckland  Bangkok  Bogotá  Buenos Aires  Calcutta
Cape Town  Chennai  Dar es Salaam  Delhi  Florence  Hong Kong  Istanbul
Karachi  Kuala Lumpur  Madrid  Melbourne  Mexico City  Mumbai
Nairobi  Paris  São Paulo  Singapore  Taipei  Tokyo  Toronto  Warsaw

with associated companies in  Berlin  Ibadan

Oxford is a registered trade mark of Oxford University Press
in the UK and in certain other countries

Hardback ISBN 0–19–910616-9
Paperback ISBN 0–19–910617-7

1 3 5 7 9 10 8 6 4 2

Printed in Spain

# Contents

▶ The mighty sea monster      4

▶ Whales are not fish      6

▶ Hunters and grazers      10

▶ Orca, the Killer whale      14

▶ The Sperm whale's battle      18

▶ The biggest animal ever      20

▶ Whale journeys      22

▶ The song of the whale      24

▶ In danger      26

▶ Glossary      30

# ▶ The mighty sea monster

In the cold, grey ocean a mighty sea monster is swimming. It rises to the surface and its sleek body slips through the waves. A fine mist spouts from the blowhole on the top of its head.

Suddenly, it leaps high out of the water. Then it falls with a great crash, sending a huge spray of water into the air. The monster flips up its tail and dives once again into the depths of the ocean.

What is the name of this sea monster?

Its name is *"**Whale**"*.

Humpback whale

#  Whales are not fish

Whales are not fish. Like us, they are mammals. Like us, they have warm blood. Like us, whale mothers carry their babies inside them until they are born.

Beluga whale
4.5 metres

dorsal fin

blowhole

Sperm whale
15 metres

**Right whale**
14 metres

**Minke whale**
8 metres

**Humpback whale**
13 metres

tail flukes

Like us, whales cannot breathe underwater. They fill their lungs, close the blowhole on the top of their heads and dive. When they surface again they breathe out through their blowhole. The warm air forms a mist of spray above their heads.

Sperm whale blowing

**Did you know...**
Most whales can stay underwater for about forty minutes but Sperm whales can stay under for up to two hours.

Like us, whales have long lives. The Sperm whale can live to seventy and Fin whales can even live until they are ninety!

But of course, whales are also very different from us. They are born in the sea. They live in the sea. They find their food in the sea.

**Did you know...**
The bones in a whale's fin are like those in a human hand.

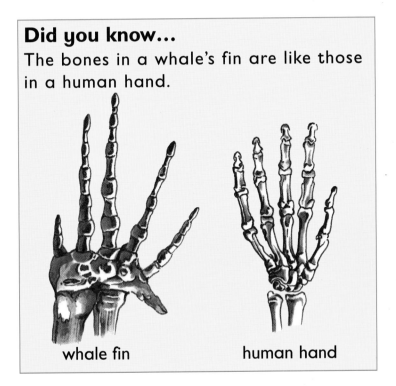

whale fin　　　　　　human hand

# Hunters and grazers

In the wild some animals, such as lions, are hunters that live by killing other creatures. Others are grazers, nibbling grass and plants all day long. Whales too are either hunters, called Toothed whales, or grazers, called Baleen whales.

Sperm whale
(Toothed whale)

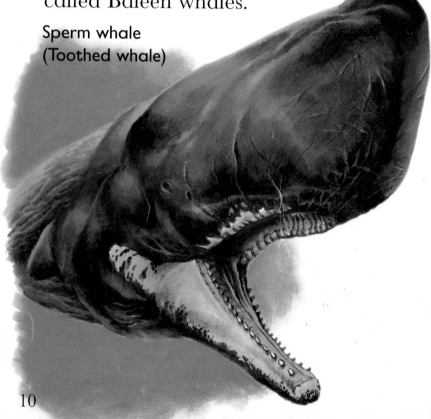

# Toothed whales

## What they eat

Mainly fish and squid. The Sperm whale eats over one thousand kilogrammes of squid a day.

## How they eat

Toothed whales have teeth for catching their prey.

## Some Toothed whales

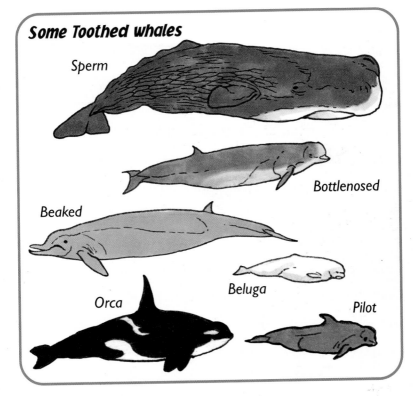

Sperm

Bottlenosed

Beaked

Beluga

Orca

Pilot

# Baleen whales

## What they eat

Millions and millions of tiny shrimp-like creatures called krill.

## How they eat

Baleen whales do not have teeth. They have strips of whalebone called "baleen" (made of the same material as cows' horns and human fingernails).

The baleen hangs from the whale's upper jaw like a thick fringe. When feeding, the whale sucks in a massive mouthful of water containing millions of krill. It then squirts the water back out through the fringe of baleen. Imagine yourself squirting water out through your teeth.

The baleen then traps the krill in the whale's mouth – and so the whale can enjoy a feast.

Bowhead whale
(Baleen whale)

## Some Baleen whales

Blue

Humpback

Bryde's

Sei

Bowhead

Grey

Finback

Minke

Right

13

# Orca, the Killer whale

The most fearsome Toothed whale is the Killer whale, Orca. With its forty-four sharp teeth, Orca eats fish, penguins, seals, sharks – and other whales.

A pod of Orcas

Orcas can swim as fast as a car driving along a street. They can leap as high as a double-decker bus.

Orcas live in family groups, called pods, of up to twenty. They often work as a team when hunting.

A group of three hungry Orcas is swimming through the Arctic Sea in search of food. They spot a seal sleeping on an ice floe.

Out of the water, the seal thinks it is safe. But it is not.

The three Orcas split up. One sneaks to the end of the floe to wait.

The other two slide under the floe and, suddenly, lift it upwards. The startled seal wakes up – but too late. The seal slides into the water and is grabbed in the jaws of the waiting Orca.

## ▶ The Sperm whale's battle

The great Sperm whale is another mighty hunter. It dives down to the bottom of the Atlantic Ocean and finds a giant squid. The squid is enormous – as long as a truck – and will be a satisfying meal for the hungry whale.

But it is also big enough to fight back.

A terrible battle takes place. The creatures struggle furiously, each fighting for its life.

At last, the Sperm whale crushes the squid in its mighty jaws.

Now it must feed and return quickly to the surface to breathe again.

# ▶ The biggest animal ever

The biggest animal ever to live on earth is not a hunter. It is a Baleen whale called the Blue whale.

A newborn Blue whale is as long as a motor boat. It drinks as much milk as fifty human families drink every day.

It takes the baby thirty years to grow to full size. It can live until it is a hundred.

**Did you know...**
The Blue whale's tongue weighs as much as a baby elephant.

Blue whale and calf

# ▶ Whale journeys

It is March and, off the coast of Mexico, over a thousand Grey whales are beginning to swim north. Their journey up the coast of America will take about three months.

As they swim, the whales will sometimes nudge and touch each other. From time to time, a mother will give her baby a piggyback.

Arriving in the Arctic they will stay until October, feeding on the rich supplies of krill. Then they will swim south again, returning to the warm waters of Mexico. Here they will breed during the winter months.

These great journeys are
called "migrations". Not all whales
migrate but, of those that do, the
Grey whale is the greatest traveller.

# ▶ The song of the whale

Deep in the ocean whales sing to each other.

Their songs are a mixture of moans, grunts, sighs, whistles and other mysterious sounds.

male Humpback whale in the head down singing position

Humpback whales are great singers. Sometimes a Humpback will go on repeating its song for a whole day and night.

Why do whales sing? Nobody really knows. However, we do know that only males sing. It is thought they sing to attract mates, to let other whales know where they are and to warn rivals to keep away.

The whale's song is one of the strangest sounds on our planet. It is also one of the most beautiful.

**Did you know...**
If you shout to a friend half a kilometre away, he or she might just hear you.
A whale can be heard as much as 80 kilometres away.

human voice
whistle blown          Humpback whale voice

| 0 km | 10 km | 20 km | 30 km | 40 km | 50 km | 60 km | 70 km | 80 km | 90 km |

# ▶ In danger

Every bit of a whale can be used.
So people have always hunted whales.

Once there were thousands of Blue whales.

Now there are only a few thousand left in the whole world.

Whale hunting is now controlled.
But whales are still in danger.
We must make everyone aware that if the whale is not saved it will surely vanish from the earth.

The whale is the biggest animal in the world yet it can't defend itself against us.

Humpback whale

In the cold blue ocean, a great and beautiful sea monster is swimming . . . it is the *mighty, wonderful whale!*

# ▶ Glossary

*This glossary will help you to understand what some important words mean. You can find them in this book by using the page numbers given below.*

 **baleen** Baleen is a fringe of whalebone that hangs from the upper jaws of those whales that have no teeth.　**10, 12, 13, 20**

 **blowhole** A blowhole is a nostril on the top of a whale's head.
**4, 6, 8**

 **breed** Breeding is when two whales mate and have a baby.
**22**

 **ice floe** An ice floe is a flat piece of ice that floats like a raft on the sea in the oceans near the North and South Poles.　**16, 17**

**krill** Krill are tiny sea creatures that look like shrimps. **12, 22**

 **mammal** Mammals are warm-blooded animals that carry their babies inside them. Both whales and humans are mammals. **6**

 **migrations** These are great journeys which whales make from one part of the oceans to another. Whales usually migrate to find food. **23**

 **pod** A pod is a small group of whales. In a pod, whales live and travel together. **14, 15**

# Reading Together

**Oxford Reds** have been written by leading children's authors who have a passion for particular non-fiction subjects. So as well as up-to-date information, fascinating facts and stunning pictures, these books provide powerful writing which draws the reader into the text.

**Oxford Reds** are written in simple language, checked by educational advisors. There is plenty of repetition of words and phrases, and all technical words are explained. They are an ideal vehicle for helping your child develop a love of reading – by building fluency, confidence and enjoyment.

You can help your child by reading the first few pages out loud, then encourage him or her to continue alone. You could share the reading by taking turns to read a page or two. Or you could read the whole book aloud, so your child knows it well before tackling it alone.

**Oxford Reds** will help your child develop a love of reading and a lasting curiosity about the world we live in.

**Sue Palmer**
*Writer and Literacy Consultant*